Whom the gods would destroy they first make psychiatrists.

—Anonymous

Psychiatry's chief contribution to philosophy is the discovery that the toilet is the seat of the soul.

—Alexander Chase

A psychoanalyst is a person who pretends he doesn't know everything.

—Anonymous

The examined life has always been pretty well confined to the privileged class.

—Edgar Friedenberg

The first step is always the hardest, but it's also the difference between moving and standing still.

—Anonymous

Anybody who goes to see a psychiatrist ought to have his head examined.

Understanding Your Therapist

or
Why Is This Taking So Long?

Robert H. Pilpel

with drawings by Stephen T. Johnson

CONTEMPORARY
BOOKS

CHICAGO · NEW YORK

Library of Congress Cataloging-in-Publication Data

Pilpel, Robert H.
    Understanding your therapist / Robert Pilpel ; with illustrations
by Stephen T. Johnson.
        p.   cm.
    ISBN 0-8092-4405-5
    1. Psychotherapist and patient.   2. Psychotherapists—
Psychology.   I. Title.
RC480.8.P55   1989
616.89′14—dc20   89-36169
                                                            CIP

Published by Contemporary Books, Inc.
180 North Michigan Avenue, Chicago, Illinois 60601
Manufactured in the United States of America
International Standard Book Number: 0-8092-4405-5

Published simultaneously in Canada by Beaverbooks, Ltd.
195 Allstate Parkway, Valleywood Business Park
Markham, Ontario L3R 4T8 Canada

CONTENTS

INTRODUCTION

LET'S FACE IT—your therapist is keeping things from you.

You know it, your therapist knows it, your castrating mother and emotionally distant father know it.

The list of things your therapist isn't telling you is virtually endless, but these are among the most commonly asked questions that he or she never answers:

- Is there any hope for me?
- How long will this whole business take?
- Will you keep seeing me if I can't keep paying you?
- Am I making good progress?
- Am I making *any* progress?
- What is your annual income?
- Where can I reach you evenings and weekends?
- Where can I reach you in August?
- Do you find me attractive?
- Shouldn't you be treating my parents instead of me?
- How do you feel about *your* parents?
- Am I your favorite patient?
- Why is this taking so long?
- Have you ever actually cured anyone?
- Have you ever even helped anyone get better?
- Who put you through graduate school?
- Are you still married to her or him?

1

- Do you make house calls?
- Are you into leather?
- Who ordered the veal cutlet?

. . . And so on.

As you can see, the questions asked in vain are well-nigh innumerable; but the responses such questions receive are pathetically few:

- Well, what do you imagine?
- Well, what comes to mind?
- Well, how do you feel about that?
- Well, time's up.

Well, enough is enough. An intolerable situation exists, one that is all too familiar to any individual who's "done time" in therapy. And this situation cries out for rectification.

It will come as no surprise to you that I, the author, have undergone therapy myself—lots and lots of it. So I know to my sorrow just how maddening it is to have the most crucial facts about my most intimate feelings kept from me for my own supposed good.

"To hell with that!" I finally decided. If one of my goals in therapy was to take charge of my life, then what better place to start taking charge than in my therapist's office? And if one of my biggest problems in therapy was my therapist's refusal to supply straightforward answers to my anguished questions, then what better response could I make than to deduce the answers for myself?

So I began to observe the very person I'd been

paying to study me—a bit timidly at first, but with ever-growing confidence as the weeks and months went by. I took note of every gesture and every nod; I assessed every grunt and evaluated every frown. After more than a year of observation, I began the slow, painstaking process of correlating each signal my therapist inadvertently sent me with subtextual inferences as to what that signal meant. I then spent another full year cross-checking and double-checking my inferences, using surreptitious trial-and-error techniques to see if I could *elicit* a particular signal from my unsuspecting therapist by means of a given verbal stimulus. If I had made a preliminary determination, for example, that a particular grunt meant "You're really *sick!*" I would announce to my therapist that I'd just spent the weekend having ménage à trois anal sex with Yasser Arafat and a Gila monster, and then see if the grunt ensued. If it did, my inference was confirmed; if it didn't, I tested another one—and so on, until I knew every signal's meaning.

When at last my researches were completed, I was astonished, quite frankly, by the magnitude of my achievement. It seemed that I had unearthed and deciphered a mysterious new language, knowledge of which might save millions of people billions of dollars and untold agonies of frustration.

But I still wasn't ready to "go public." I first wanted to establish that my findings were applicable not just to my therapist but to all therapists without exception. So I spent one final, arduous year testing out my results on a statistically selected cross-section of therapists in New York City, Beverly Hills, Zurich, Vienna, Portuguese Macao, Vatican City, and the United Arab Emirates.

The outcome of my verification studies was intensely gratifying, and I am proud to announce that my findings have been confirmed down to the smallest detail. They have been demonstrated, moreover, to possess not merely intrinsic accuracy but cross-cultural validity as well. Indeed, the insights provided in this book have been so thoroughly corroborated that neurotics all over the world will now be able to complete a standard seven-year analysis in a maximum of nine weeks (assuming no missed sessions).

I conclude, therefore, with the perhaps immodest assertion that my discoveries represent the greatest single contribution to mental health since the invention of K-Y Jelly. And it is with a deep and abiding sense of avarice that I now release them to the world.

21 May 1989
Evades-les-Taxxez
Valais Canton,
Switzerland

4

THE FIRST SESSION

IN YOUR FIRST ENCOUNTER with your therapist, be as observant as possible. Notice the subtle things. Is the therapist conscious? Is he fully clothed? Details like these may seem unimportant to begin with, but they can have a significant incremental impact over the years.

Take note, also, of your therapist's working arrangements. Is his office inside a building? If so, is the building on fire? Is there furniture in her consulting room? Is the room carpeted? Is the furniture carpeted? Are facilities for the patients located inside the building? How about a hockey rink?

Next be aware of how your therapist relates to you. Does she permit you to sit down? To talk without raising your hand? Must you wear a uniform? Must you recite the Pledge of Allegiance?

Now observe your therapist's manner. Is she relaxed, or has she barricaded herself behind a bunker? Is the bunker carpeted? Does he give you eye contact, or has he plucked out his own eyes because he killed his father and married his mother?

Finally, focus on what your therapist says. Does it resonate with your own preconscious perceptions, or indicate contempt for everything you stand for, or both? Does it inspire you to take control of your life or suggest that, in your case, the less self-knowledge the better? Most important, does it make sense? If the answer is yes, there's no doubt you can benefit from therapy. If the answer is no, welcome to the club!

THE STANDARD EXPRESSION OF TERMINAL THERAPEUTIC NEUTRALITY

THIS IS THE therapist's way of saying Hi!

This is also the therapist's way of saying 'Bye!

From the therapist's point of view, in fact, this is the ideal way to say *everything* and the ideal way to look whenever in conference with a patient. A full four months of graduate school training are devoted to the cultivation and maintenance of this expression. That is why therapists are so eagerly sought after by directors of horror movies like *Night of the Living Dead* and *Invasion of the Body Snatchers*.

On this blank screen, the hapless patient is induced to project all his neuroses, without being distracted by any aspect of the therapist's personality.

That is one reason so many neurotic people are often seen talking to themselves.

THE INSUFFERABLY PATRONIZING SMILE

THE INSUFFERABLY PATRONIZING SMILE ranks second in importance only to the SE-of-TTN in the therapist's arsenal of facial expressions.* It serves a very specific therapeutic purpose: the liberation of repressed anger. Not even the most anally retentive precatatonic sulker can withstand fifty minutes of concentrated IPS provocation without venting some of his rage. That is why most adept IPS-ers prefer to consult with their patients while seated in a well-built shark cage, psychiatric versions of which have been adapted from underwater research models (available postpaid from Frederick's of Hollywood and other medical supply houses).

---

*Because of the risks involved in its use, IPS training is available only to middle-aged clergy with bad teeth and to physicians who have completed at least three years of a psychiatric residency. Use of the IPS in non-therapeutic environments, such as ICBM silos and Weight Watchers meetings, is specifically "Not Recommended" by both the American Medical Association and the National Conference of Christians and Jews.

"I CAN'T TELL YOU WHAT TO FEEL"

THIS PHRASE MEANS "Shmuck! You're still not feeling what I keep telling you to feel!" It is used whenever a patient is incautious enough to report any feelings other than murderous rage or convulsive guilt, and insecure enough to ask her therapist if such nonstandard emotions are "appropriate."*

"I Can't Tell You What to Feel" can have any of several more specific meanings, depending on the therapeutic context. Inter alia, the phrase can mean:

- You're afraid to admit what you're really feeling, shmuck!
- You're afraid to feel what you're really feeling, shmuck!
- What you think you're feeling isn't what you're really feeling, shmuck!
- What you're afraid to admit you think you're feeling isn't what you really think you're admitting you're afraid to think about feeling, poopsie!**

---

*Patients reporting feelings of murderous rage or convulsive guilt are rewarded with the Noncommittal Nod Connoting Approval. See page 28.

**In the event your therapist is a Gentile, substitute "peckerhead" for "shmuck," and "babycakes" for "poopsie."

THE THROAT CLEAR

BE ON YOUR TOES WHEN your therapist clears his throat; it means he is processing an impulse to spit in your face. Of course, his professionalism will influence him to refrain from giving effect to the impulse, most of the time. But it's always wise to prepare for the occasional lapse.

Why, you ask, should my therapist be entertaining an impulse to spit in my face? Well, think of all the secrets you've confided over the course of your treatment—the confessions of impure thoughts, unspeakable hatreds, loathsome vices, and poor oral hygiene. Naturally your therapist maintains the pretense that his professional detachment keeps him from responding emotionally to the beast that lurks beneath your mealy-mouthed exterior. But he is only mortal, in most cases, and sooner or later the realization that he is dealing with someone so depraved, so selfish, so overweight, and so poorly dressed will overcome even his most deep-seated professional scruples.

Well, then, how can you realistically defend yourself? Many patients find that wearing full scuba gear during sessions not only protects them against sudden expectoration but greatly improves their tennis game. Other therapees find that a motorcycle helmet and visor provide an ample margin of safety. My own preference is to bring a fully loaded sidearm to every session.

THE APPARENT DOZE

THE APPARENT DOZE IS merely the Standard Expression of Terminal Therapeutic Neutrality as seen by the patient when the therapist's eyes are closed. Contrary to near unanimous patient opinion, the Apparent Doze does *not* mean that the therapist has fallen asleep.

"I have *never*, EVER dozed off in the presence of a client," declared one representative practitioner I interviewed. "Not for one second have I napped. Not even while some regressed bozo is droning on about his urge to slit his wrists. One of the first things I learned in therapy school was that, no matter what, I had to keep awake and alert at all times. Why? Because if a therapist takes his eyes off a patient for even an instant, he leaves his own genitalia vulnerable to attack!"

"Well, then," I asked the anxious-looking doctor, "what *is* the true significance of the Apparent Doze?"

"Just tell your readers," he replied, "that the therapist is trying to present the patient with a reassuring image of benign impassivity. . . . But be sure to add that all of us in the therapy biz have had trâining in the martial arts."*

---

*Although most of the therapists I interviewed subscribe to this point of view, a significant minority see things from a different perspective. "The Apparent Doze means that your therapist trusts you enough to let you do some of your analyzing 'solo,' so to speak," one of them explained to me. "It's really the highest form of compliment, and the appropriate patient response is simply to place your check on the therapist's knee and make as little noise as possible when you leave."

THE DR. RUTH TWINKLE

THE DR. RUTH TWINKLE IS a two-edged sword, or words to that effect. Its appearance indicates that your therapist finds you adorable and loves you to small pieces. This is not a bad thing in and of itself, but neither is it necessarily a good thing. If you are a middle-aged man, for example, the emergence of the Dr. Ruth Twinkle on your therapist's face will strike you one way if the therapist is a thirty-year-old cross between Hedy Lamarr and Mamie Van Doren, and quite another if she resembles Bigfoot.

Of course, whatever you are and whatever your therapist is, the coming of the Dr. Ruth Twinkle tells you that your therapist has become emotionally attached to you. And this raises a nice point of professional ethics. For therapists not only are supposed to maintain their therapeutic objectivity, but have a concomitant obligation to withdraw from all cases where objectivity proves impossible.

What will your therapist do?

Well, either way, you win. If the idea of a nontherapeutic meaningful relationship with your therapist appeals to you (as it should, if you're serious about your therapy), an ethical offer to refer you to another practitioner should immediately start you thinking about marriage, or whatever. An unethical readiness to continue as before entitles you, on the other hand, to dive into one of those mutually exploitive game-playing

relationships that always ends badly after truckloads of great sex.

If the idea of a non-therapeutic meaningful relationship with your therapist does not appeal to you, then you do not take your therapy seriously, and the therapist's ethics are irrelevant. Unless, of course, you're interested in engaging in blackmail or psychic torture.

In which case you might want to consider a career in public service.

THE FROWN OF CONCENTRATION AND THE FROWN OF CONSTIPATION

IT IS VITALLY IMPORTANT to distinguish between these two easily confused expressions, because they mean entirely different things. Interpreting a Frown of Concentration as a Frown of Constipation can strain your relationship with your therapist; interpreting a Frown of Constipation as a Frown of Concentration can turn that relationship into a quagmire.

Basically, the Frown of Concentration is a GOOD sign, and the Frown of Constipation is a DANGER sign. A nifty way to keep the two frowns straight in your mind is to remember that orange juice—one of life's GOOD things—is concentrated, while cinder blocks—a common metaphor for constipation—pose great DANGER when dropped out of airplanes onto busy midtown intersections.

The Frown of Concentration is a GOOD sign because it means roughly the same thing as the Deeply Concerned Forward Lean (see page 26). It means, in other words, that you've finally gotten your therapist's attention (unless, of course, he's concentrating on something other than you—a possibility you might want to consider if he's wearing earphones, say, or engaging in self-abuse).

The Frown of Constipation is a DANGER sign because it means you are talking about something that

makes the therapist feel anally fixated, obsessed with making money, deficient in dietary fiber, and Gentile (see Glossary).

Now it's easy to understand the importance of distinguishing between these two frowns. The obvious response to the Frown of Concentration is to keep on talking about the subject that elicited it, preferably in the same sulky tone of voice. The proper response to the Frown of Constipation, on the other hand, is to shift immediately from the topic you've been discussing to one that involves frequent references to prunes and whole-grain cereals.

If the unthinkable happens and you get the two frowns mixed up, the consequences can be appalling. By suddenly launching into a gushy appreciation of organically grown laxatives when your therapist is merely frowning in concentration, for instance, you not only disrupt his therapeutic flow but raise questions in his mind as to whether you can ever truly be helped. And by misguidedly sulking along about the same old subject when his frown is in fact one of constipation, you render him steadily more susceptible to the aforementioned feelings of fixation, obsession, and deficiency, to the point where he may even vote Republican.

Given such grisly possibilities, it is essential to take note of the telltale signs that indicate which of the two frowns you are confronting. As you might expect, if the therapist has his legs, arms, fingers, and/or eyes crossed, or has inserted one or more of his fingers into one or more of his bodily orifices, then constipation is almost certainly afoot. By contrast, you can feel confident that your therapist is simply concentrating if he appears alert, responsive, and at ease, or is wearing disposable diapers.

THE CHAIR OR THE COUCH

AS THE AUTHOR OF THIS BOOK, I can't pretend to be objective about the chair-couch dichotomy. Almost all therapists who favor the couch sit out of their patient's line of sight, which means that their facial expressions and body language go unobserved. I mean, what's the sense talking?

My bias aside, however, what are the merits of the couch? According to Freudian theory, it keeps a patient's stream of consciousness free of the distracting external input that goes with face-to-face interaction. It also allows the therapist to pick his nose without being observed (see The Nose Pick).

Looked at impartially, both of these rationales seem pretty flimsy. The proper response, in my opinion, is to wait till your therapist is asleep (see The Apparent Doze) and then attach one of those miniature rearview mirrors to your eyeglass frames. (If you don't wear eyeglasses, you don't need therapy, and the couch/chair controversy becomes moot.) Even if your therapist wakes up before the end of the session, he'll be too busy picking his nose to notice what you've done, and you'll be able to watch him as carefully as you wish.

True, many patients would rather not look at their therapist's face, ever, believing as they do that mortal eyes were never meant to gaze upon His/Her shining countenance. Such patients tend to congregate on the grounds of the U.S. embassy in Tehran.

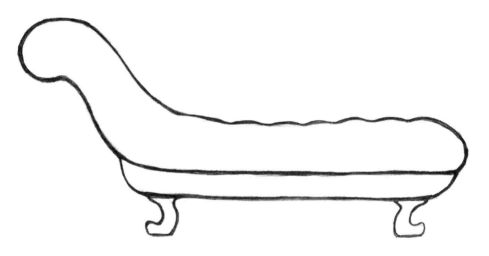

THE FREE-ASSOCIATIVE FART

THIS IS ONE OF THE MOST significant noises a therapist can make. Far from being a mere gastrointestinal happenstance, it is as revealing, and eloquent, a comment as is ever likely to issue from your therapist's . . . person.

Although the precise meaning of an episode of audible flatulence will depend on the subject under discussion at the time, the interjection's general import may be summarized as follows:

If the F-A-Fer is . . .	then the F-A-F means . . .
a Freudian	the therapist owns an accordian.
a Jungian	you are making the therapist feel powerful.
a Gestalt-ian	the therapist wants to share his essence with you.
a Transactional Analyst	the therapist's Child is angry at your Parent.
a Social Worker	the therapist is living on a diet of baked beans.

"WHAT'S MORE IMPORTANT—
A WEEK IN THE BAHAMAS OR
THE REST OF YOUR LIFE?"

THE MESSAGE IMPLICIT IN this stock expression—that the patient's entire life will disintegrate if he skips a few appointments—is viewed by some fainthearted therapists as dishonest, coercive, self-serving, and mercenary.

Who did they ever cure?!

The fact is that very few therapists have any intention of manipulating their patients when using this expression. Being of a philosophical bent for the most part, they are simply posing a deep metaphysical question for their patients to consider. And, believe it or not, the answer to that question is, in existential terms, by no means obvious. Given the right contacts, a week in the Bahamas could turn out to be very important indeed, while the rest of many lives is usually pretty trivial.

So what the therapist really means when he raises the issue is that the patient should either alter his life dramatically or make reservations at a better hotel.

Who among us would not benefit from confronting such a choice?

THE VOMIT

THIS IS A HIGHLY ambiguous signal.

Of course, most people in therapy instantly assume its meaning is transparently clear. They think it confirms their long-held suspicions that the therapist finds their innermost souls acutely nauseating.

In fact, the full syrupy meaning of the Vomit is far more complicated.

"Puking is sharing," as Freud observed while wiping partially digested morsels of knackwurst off his wife's bullwhip. And his disciples Jung and Adler both viewed "patient-centered regurgitation" as a key stimulus in the development of primary transference (see Glossary).

The Vomit, therefore, should be viewed as an invitation to reveal more of oneself, just as the therapist is doing. And, of course you share the wastebasket.

But throwing up is a uniquely individual means of self-expression. Here, nuance is everything. If your therapist's cheeks bulge just before he goes "whoops," for example, he's mimicking your efforts to keep your feelings repressed. (He may also be making fun of your fat cheeks.) If he makes loud retching noises in the act of heaving, he's saying that your resistance to self-revelation is keeping you so far from him, psychologically speaking, that he almost has to shout to be heard. (He may also be saying that he's worried you're not hearing him because your cheeks are so fat they're blocking your ears.) If he vomits directly on you, he's attempting to provoke you into a sudden cathartic

expression of your repressed feelings, particularly the shame you've always felt because your cheeks are so fat.

The reliability of the interpretations is contingent, so be sure to check for signs of biliousness. If the therapist is acting queasy and making mournful animal noises, a regurgitative episode should *not* lead you to lower your guard. It simply means the therapist has an intestinal virus, which has made him realize he finds your inner-most soul acutely nauseating.

THE DEEPLY CONCERNED
FORWARD LEAN
(HANDS CLASPED, ELBOWS ON KNEES)

THIS PARTICULAR BODY configuration should be music to every patient's eyes, because it indicates that you have finally succeeded in getting your therapist interested in what you are saying. The wise patient will take advantage of this signal by noting immediately: (1) the subject you are obsessing about at that moment, and (2) the degree of whininess in your voice.

Armed with these two pieces of information, you will henceforth be in a position to combat such depressing symptoms of therapist boredom as the Apparent Doze and the Apparent Yawn. In fact, whenever your therapist's mind seems to wander, you can reclaim the attention you're paying for by simply reverting to the topic and whine-pitch that calls forth the DCFL (HC,EOK).*

---

*Patients in the early stages of therapy would be well advised to make deliberate efforts to induce DCFL (HC,EOK) behavior in their therapists. The knowledge obtained will save innumerable hours and dollars. Unfortunately, there are no surefire DCFL (HC,EOK) topics, but any list of the most promising ones (with associated whine-pitch) would have to include: (1) how I wipe myself (whimper); (2) my most disgusting sex fantasies (snivel); (3) the last time I saw my mother or father naked (hiccup); and (4) why I prefer the Old Testament (snigger).

THE NONCOMMITTAL NOD CONNOTING APPROVAL

THIS, OF COURSE, IS SIMPLY another way of describing the barely perceptible up-and-down motion of a face displaying the Standard Expression of Terminal Therapeutic Neutrality. Unlike the SE of TTN, however, the NCNCA is highly revealing of the therapist's inner thoughts, and it has therefore been classified as an "unprofessional treatment technique" by COUCH, the Council for Overseeing, Upgrading, and Cross-ventilating tHerapeutic practice. Therapists who cannot rid themselves of this half-conscious mannerism—even after repeated motivational beatings at the hands of COUCH "Nod Squads"—must undergo the surgical implantation of a transparent neck brace, which permits only side-to-side motion of the head. Although this somewhat drastic remedy tends, among other things, to reduce the number of therapists attending air and dog shows, the stakes are so high that both society as a whole and the entire therapeutic profession are willing to pay the price.

Given the crucial importance of the information conveyed by the NCNCA, the draconian response of the therapy establishment becomes understandable. For the NCNCA means nothing less than, "You're on the right track, you're making sense, you're achieving insight" (see Glossary). If, therefore, your therapist has thus far eluded the COUCH dragnet, you have a golden opportunity to improve your mental health at a

breathtaking pace. If your therapist has already been broken of the NCNCA habit, on the other hand, you'll have to make do with the Deeply Concerned Forward Lean and the Frown of Concentration.

Alternatively, you can change therapists.

"WHAT COMES TO MIND?"

THIS STOCK EXPRESSION is designed to help your therapist gain insight into your unconscious. Its use is grounded on the fundamental therapeutic tenet that there is nothing random about the patterns of thought and emotion that constitute our mental experience. In other words, everything that comes to mind reveals the mind. In a simple word association sequence, for example, if you said, "Dog," and I responded, "From the rear," an observant therapist would conclude right away that you were seriously disturbed. No one in his right mind walks up to other people and says things like "Dog." For some reason you do, however, and any therapist worth his salt can use that fact to achieve greater understanding of your personality.

"What Comes to Mind?" then, is simply your therapist's professionally sanctioned way of saying, "Dog." You should respond, "From the rear," whenever the question is asked. This will influence your therapist to stop asking the question. And before you know it, you will have rid yourself of one of the most irritating features of psychotherapy.

THERAPISTS' VACATIONS

YOUR THERAPIST TAKES TWO categories of vacations—Discretionary and Mandatory. The Discretionary includes the standard month of August along with stretches around the new year and vernal equinox. The Mandatory are those taken concurrently with climactic crises in your personal life. Sometimes, of course, the two categories may overlap, as when a climactic crisis in your personal life coincides with the vernal equinox. The fact that such a vacation coincides with a crisis puts it squarely into the Mandatory category.

The COUCH Committee On Patient Torment (COPTOR) has been emphatic about this matter, to the point where some therapists who've attempted to cancel what they believed to be Discretionary vacations have been compelled to go off on their holidays against their will.

"It's mostly an administrative expedient," explains COPTOR chair Dr. Joel Snizle. "Ultraneedy patients are a real turnoff, and we think our therapists have to get away from them till they calm down. Sure, it's hard on a few people, but the therapists are almost always grateful to us afterward."

And the abandoned patients?

"They do fine," says Snizle. "They eventually stop whimpering and settle down for a nice long stare into space."

33

THE DROOLING LEER

THIS IS A HIGHLY INFORMATIVE signal, which can prove to be of enormous value to the patient. While on a superficial level it may mean only that your fly is open or your blouse unbuttoned, it can be of monumental significance if your garments are properly fastened.

Not to put too fine a point on it, the appearance of the Drooling Leer on your therapist's face is usually an indication that he or she may be having some difficulty retaining his or her professional objectivity.

Now, there's no reason to panic. Remain calm, hand the therapist paper towels, and whisper, "countertransference" (see Glossary).* Once the therapist regains composure, the two of you can work together to relate the just concluded fluctuation in therapeutic demeanor to the material (see Glossary) you were discussing when he or she began behaving like an animal.

Since the threat of public exposure and professional humiliation is a powerful bargaining chip, you should be able to count on free therapy for at least a month after any session involving the Drooling Leer. If you succeed in figuring out exactly what it was that triggered the therapist's arousal, moreover, the knowledge gained will prove invaluable when you're well enough to start livening up your social life.

---

*Not "countertransference (see Glossary)," as this will only make things worse.

THE NOSE PICK

LET ME BEGIN BY APOLOGIZING. The business of analyzing this therapist activity is as distasteful to me as it is to you. Writing as a dedicated social scientist, however, I feel an obligation to describe observed phenomena as they are, without flinching or prettifying.

Proceeding in that spirit, I can say that one likely meaning of the Nose Pick is that your therapist has a monster booger in one or both nostrils.

But that, of course, is seldom the whole story.

Let's face it, therapists themselves will tell you that the insertion of a jointed probe into a bodily orifice has powerful symbolic significance. The act, indeed, is even more symbolic than the act it symbolizes.

What then does your therapist mean by the Nose Pick? The obvious message—that his sinuses are clogged—may reflect the true situation. But the underlying message is even more important. Where is the therapist's finger, after all? Inside his head. And in what direction is it moving? Why, toward his brain.

Now, the meaning of the Nose Pick becomes evident: the therapist is relieving a sensation of pruritis in his organ of mentation by means of digital palpation, i.e. your therapist's brain itches, and he is scratching it.

Thus, the correct interpretation of the Nose Pick is that your therapist needs to have his brain shampooed or reupholstered.

Thank you for your attention.

PAYING YOUR THERAPIST

MOST THERAPISTS PREFER to be paid in Krugerrands, but the currency you use is far less important than its dollar-equivalent. Also far less important than its dollar-equivalent is the form and frequency of payment. But if you pay in cash, be sure to tender crisp, new bills in correct serial number sequence. This is very important to therapists, who have a horror of old, wrinkled paper money, ones in particular.

Nor should the denomination of the bills you proffer be left to chance. Fifties are considered ostentatious and may prompt your therapist to downgrade your prognosis. Ones, of course, are beneath his notice. Fives have become the hip denomination among younger therapists, largely because most automatic teller machines dispense only tens and twenties. However commonplace, these last two denominations are also acceptable. But they do not make a good impression over the long term.

Almost all therapists will accept payment by check. But the check should always be written before you arrive for your session. Writing a check while inside your therapist's office is considered gauche in the extreme; entering the transaction in your checkbook in the therapist's presence may seriously jeopardize your continued access to psychotropic medications.

And for God's sake, write neatly!

Payment by credit card is gaining acceptance among many psychotherapeutic practitioners. Note, however, that any card bonuses, such as frequent-flyer miles or merchandise discounts, must be split fifty-fifty. And please be patient while your therapist telephones for the charge authorization.

Finally, there is barter. If you have an exceptional skill or figure, your therapist may be willing to do a little horse-trading with respect to your fee. You might cook him a gourmet meal, for example, or bring him to orgasm. The important thing to remember is that everything's negotiable.

Now as to frequency of payment. The custom of the trade dictates monthly billing but some therapists will accept payment on a session-by-session basis. When they do, they are entitled to tack on a surcharge.

A few of the more entrepreneurial practitioners offer therapy at no risk or obligation. If, as one of their patients, you are not completely satisfied with any given session, you pay absolutely nothing! Simply disregard any insights and write "cancel" on your bill. By the same token, of course, you'll be charged extra for any sessions that make you a better person.

THE NYAH-nyah-nyah-NYAH-NYAH TOUGUE FLICK

THERE ARE TWO (2) SCHOOLS of thought with regard to the N-N-N-N-NTF. One, the Transactional view, interprets the behavior as a reflex regressive response to any bad consequences that result from a patient's failure to follow the therapist's advice. It's a therapeutic way of saying, "I told you so, dork!" And it reflects imperfectly sublimated (see Glossary) feelings of frustration and anger arising from the patient's disobedience.

The second, or Freudian, view is that the N-N-N-N-NTF is the sadomasochistic (do *not* see Glossary) reaction formation (see Glossary) occasioned by the same stimulus. The therapist is sexually aroused (I *love* when you disobey me and it costs you!) and at the same time infuriated (How *dare* you disobey me when I was right for once!). And by engaging in N-N-N-N-NTF behavior, he/she manages, in a relatively harmless way, to express both the eroticism (flicking tongue) and the rage (NYAH-nyah-nyah-NYAH-NYAH) he/she is feeling.

But what if your therapist engages in N-N-N-N-NTF behavior even though you always follow his/her advice? The only possible explanation is that your therapist is less than twelve years old and thinks you're a fool for taking advice from a kid. Either that, or your therapist is Morton Downey, Jr.

41

THE NONCOMMITTAL NOD
CONNOTING DISAPPROVAL

HERE, AS WITH THE NCNCA, we are dealing with the Standard Expression of Terminal Therapeutic Neutrality in motion. In contrast with the NCNCA's up-and-down movement, however, the NCNCD features a side-to-side oscillation. And because it connotes merely a negative reaction to the patient, COUCH does not regard it as a threat to the integrity of the therapeutic process.

"Of course, we'd prefer that our therapists maintain a terminally neutral facade at all times," comments Dr. Bella Krotch, chair of COUCH's Enforcement Committee. "But if a practitioner occasionally lets slip some hint that he regards the patient with contempt, well, we can understand his point of view."

Usually the disapproval connoted by the NCNCD is of a relatively mild sort, relating, say, to mismatched accessories, poor penmanship on a check, or your fat cheeks. Sometimes, though—when it conveys disdain or something stronger—it is a reaction to the material you're presenting at the time it appears. Nine times out of ten, it simply means, "Get to the dirty stuff already!" Which is to say, you are focusing on material unrelated to sex and excretion, and the therapist is becoming understandably impatient. One time out of ten, it means, "You disgust me!" Which signifies that you

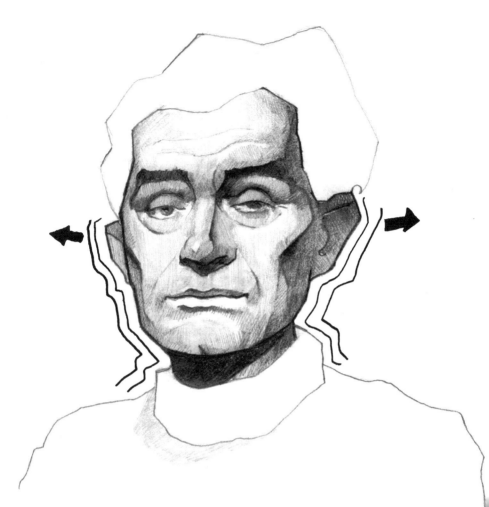

have overcompensated (see Glossary) for the other nine times.

The proper response to the NCNCD, therefore, is to either start (90 percent of the time) or stop (the other 12 percent of the time) talking dirty—unless, of course, you enjoy disgusting your therapist and/or making him feel impatient. In that case, you are rapidly approaching a state of mental health.

THE DEFECATORY SQUAT

THE ASSUMPTION OF THIS POSITION by your therapist should always be taken seriously, especially if you're not wearing waders. At best, it indicates that your therapist is suffering from an intestinal virus. At worst, it is a commentary on your worth as a human being. In the middle range of cases, it is a commentary on your worth as an intestinal virus.

What in heaven's name could provoke therapists to indulge in this kind of behavior when they aren't suffering from an intestinal virus? To understand the answer to that question, we need to go back to Vienna in the early 1900s. There, in a small apartment by the Seine, Sigmund Freud began his exploration of the unconscious. It wasn't easy during those early years (of the 1900s), and, like many people who spend most of their time in a seated position, Freud began to experience symptoms that make even our darkest fantasies look like first communions.

Being a man of action as well as contemplation, Freud contacted his exercise therapist, Baron von Krafft-Ebing, who advised him to stretch his gluteal muscles at every opportunity. Imagine the great analyst's surprise when one of his patients actually rose from the couch while Freud was stretching his gluteals and said, "Doc, I've gotta be going now." This incident convinced Freud that Krafft-Ebing was a lousy exercise

therapist, and of course it was Friedrich Nietzsche who eventually took over from the Baron.

But Nietzsche was suffering from an intestinal virus at that time, largely because of his recent death. So rather than tell Freud to stop stretching his gluteals in the presence of his patients, Nietzsche simply presented him with a commentary on his patients' worth as human beings. This led Freud to write his greatest psychoanalytic treatise, *Power Bowling*.

In the decades since Freud and Nietzsche collaborated, generations of therapists have come and gone. But the master's tradition of stretching one's gluteal muscles during therapy sessions still lives on among the more orthodox practitioners.

That is why the Defecatory Squat should always be taken seriously. And what you should always say by way of response is, "Doc, I gotta be going now."

THE BELCH

LIKE THE FREE-ASSOCIATIVE FART, the Belch is an expulsion of gas from the alimentary canal. And like the Vomit, it involves a reversal of the normal direction of flow within the digestive tract. Thus, the Belch may be thought of as the act of vomiting gas, and therein lies its meaning. For what is it that immediately comes to mind when we think of gas? Why, self-service, of course. And what is it that immediately comes to mind when we think of vomiting? You guessed it! Cleaning up the mess. What your therapist is saying with the Belch, in other words, is that you can accumulate sufficient energy to clean up the mess you've made of your life if you will only pump the fuel of insight into the gas tank of your ego instead of just waiting around for someone to clean the dead bugs off your windshield.

What your therapist is revealing, in essence, is that you really don't need therapy; and the very idea perturbs his gastric juices to the point where they froth up and generate large volumes of bilious vapors.

The Belch, in the final analysis, is the signal you've always dreaded: you're unhappy not because you're neurotic, but because you've got a lot to be unhappy about.

Now you understand why most people prefer to be neurotic.

47

THE TITTER

OF COURSE, IT'S NOT the Titter per se that matters but the context in which the Titter occurs. The Titter that escapes your therapist when you tell her she reminds you of your mother, for example, means something altogether different from the Titter she utters when you tell her you want her right now, on the floor! In the former instance, your therapist is revealing embarrassment over the fact that in your mind she has come to stand for the poor woman you've been reviling nonstop for the past nine years. In the latter instance, your therapist is revealing that you bring out the animal in her and that she wishes she'd had her office carpeted.

"But what if my therapist is a man?" you ask. (As if anyone who titters could ever be a real man.) Well, if you also are a man, your tittering therapist is thinking, "Funny, you remind me of your mother, too." If you are a woman, the Titter of a male practitioner is a sure sign that his hourly fees, among other things, are about to rise.

Why? Because he's going to have to pay a bundle for all that brand-new office carpeting.

USING YOUR THERAPIST'S FACILITIES

ALL THERAPISTS PROVIDE their patients with ready access to toilet facilities, for reasons you can deduce for yourself if you're fixated on that sort of thing. But, knowing their patients as they do, the therapists never use such facilities themselves, preferring the nearest bus station or legislature.

Using your therapist's facilities therefore exposes you to no risk of therapeutic molestation. This doesn't mean it's an altogether risk-free enterprise, however, given the endless procession of neurotics who've gone to the designated room before you and who will surely continue to come after.

Rule 1, accordingly, is: do not attempt to use your therapist's facilities at the same time other patients are using them. Although it's a commendable way of conserving water, the risks involved are unacceptable.

Rule 2 is a corollary of Rule 1: immediately upon entering the room that houses your therapist's facilities, shut the door behind you and make sure it's secure against forced entry. A few two-by-fours nailed across the door frame should provide an adequate margin of safety, unless your therapist's clientele includes heterosexuals.

Rule 3: your therapist is always out of toilet paper.

Rule 4 states the optimum strategy for dealing with calls of nature at your therapist's office: get yourself to the nearest bus station!

THE LIP-WETTING TONGUE FLICK

THIS FACIAL EXPRESSION tells you that you are in serious danger, because it means that your therapist thinks she is Wiliam F. Buckley, Jr. Under certain circumstances, it might even mean that your therapist *is* William F. Buckley, Jr.

The danger you face, if your therapist believes herself to be William F. Buckley, Jr., is most acute if she is a woman. Because Bill Buckley, for all his faults, is still beyond doubt of the male sex. Thus a female therapist who believes herself to be him is doubly deluded.

But why does that pose a danger to the patient? Well, what kind of therapeutic advice will a woman who thinks she's Bill Buckley be most likely to give?

Precisely.

And a male therapist who thinks he's Bill Buckley won't do that much better.

Of course, if your therapist actually *is* Bill Buckley, and you weren't born rich, then you face an entirely different threat.

All in all, the Lip-Wetting Tongue Flick should be your signal to reevaluate your relationship with your therapist and start subscribing to the *National Review*.

Because Bill Buckley never promised you a rose garden.

51

THE DANDRUFF SCRATCH

CONTRARY TO WHAT you might suppose, the Dandruff Scratch does not indicate that your therapist is deficient with regard to personal hygiene. Dandruff is a dermatological condition unrelated to the cleanliness of the scalp. Indeed, hair that is cleansed too often may be more susceptible to dandruff than the chronically dirty hair. Indoor dryness during the colder months may aggravate the condition, and the so-called dandruff shampoos do little to diminish flaking. In earlier times, numerous home remedies were developed to deal with dandruff—washing the hair with egg whites, beer, and lemon juice, for example. But it wasn't until the 1980s that the science of dermatology first achieved a thorough understanding of the affliction. That is why we as a nation can at long last look forward to the conquest of flaky scalp.

THE INSUFFERABLY
SELF-SATISFIED CHORTLE

UNLIKE THE INSUFFERABLY patronizing smile, the Insufferably Self-Satisfied Chortle is not intended to provoke the patient to anger. In fact, it has no underlying motivation whatsoever. It is merely a natural manifestation of insufferable self-satisfaction.

The IS-SC is usually elicited by patients protesting the ground rules of the therapeutic relationship. For example, "Why won't you ever just give me a little good advice?!" is a surefire cue for the IS-SC. Indeed, some therapists have been known to burst into insufferably self-satisfied guffaws when asked this question.

Why therapists react to their patients' declarations of exasperation with attacks of acute complacency is a question that has fascinated proctologists for centuries. One school of thought holds that the self-satisfaction is a defense against feelings of anxiety aroused by signs of patient rebellion. Another school believes that it stems from feelings of superiority arising from the fact that the therapist is not in therapy himself.

Whatever the root cause of this virtually reflex response, it invariably engenders strong homicidal tendencies in the patients subjected to it. COUCH, accordingly, has organized Chortle Alert to keep its member therapists from harm. A combination electrode/antenna implanted in the therapist's diaphragm picks up chortles and transmits an alarm to Chortle Central on

Manhattan's Upper West Side. Within seconds, a highly trained quick-response team made up of folk dancers, manicurists, and the University of Southern California Trojan Marching Band is on its way to the endangered therapist's office. Once the team arrives, the manicurists keep the patient's hands occupied, while the folk dancers force him if not her to follow their steps as the University of Southern California Trojan Marching Band plays "Mayim," an Israeli song in praise of water(?). The team's intervention distracts and constrains the patient while awakening healing ethnic memories in the therapist.

Though COUCH is justifiably proud of Chortle Central's record of rescues, it still relies on therapists themselves to keep their chortles to a minimum. As Dr. Bella Krotch insightfully observed, "It's one thing to know you're better than your patient; it's quite another thing to flaunt your superiority openly. We recommend that you flaunt it surreptitiously. In other words, whenever you feel a chortle coming on, you should immediately raise your hourly fees."

"DID YOU HEAR WHAT YOU JUST SAID?"

THIS QUESTION OFTEN MEANS that the therapist wasn't paying attention. If you *did* hear what you just said and are then told to, "Repeat what you just said," you can be reasonably sure that this is the case. If you wish to get back at your therapist, announce that you will write down what you just said if he/she will write it down, too. This will cause the therapist to ask, "Why are you resisting?"—to which the proper response is, "Why aren't you paying attention, shmuck?!"

But there are times when "Did you hear what you just said?" signals a therapist's belief that the words you spoke are more significant than you realize. You may have uddered a Freudian Slip (see Glossary), or even have illuminated a darkened region of your psyche.

Often, the statement that elicits "Did You Hear What You Just Said?" is marked by gross incompatibility with the accompanying emotions. If you are jabbing pins into dolls that represent your parents, for example, and declaring in the process that as you enter your late thirties your mother and father mean more to you than wealth, fame, and the love of beautiful persons, your therapist will almost certainly ask the question.

On balance, therefore, "Did You Hear What You Just Said?" means that your therapist is either on the case or goofing off. If you burst into tears when the question is asked and discover that you can walk again, it's probably the former. If you have any other reaction, make sure you have paper and pencil handy.

"WHY ARE YOU RESISTING?"

THIS QUESTION IS the psychotherapeutic equivalent of "Stop dogging it, bozo!" It is based on the theory that people often seek to avoid the painful feelings stirred up in therapy by becoming distracted, losing focus, refusing to comprehend, or requesting a sex-change operation. The reprimand implicit in "Why Are You Resisting?" is phrased as a question pursuant to COUCH guidelines, which classify statements like "Stop dogging it, bozo!" as incompatible with a patient's disposition to make regular payments.

If, like most therapees, you have been doing your darndest to derive at least some meager insight from your dialogues with your therapist, the question "Why Are You Resisting?" should really piss you off (see Glossary). Appropriate responses include:

- Because you're so resistible.
- What's it to you?
- Why am I resisting what?
- Who are you calling a bozo?
- So's your mother.

If none of these seems appropriate, a sex-change operation is probably the way to go.

THE RABID SNARL

SAFETY FIRST IS THE WATCHWORD in all psychother-apeutic situations, from simple counseling sessions to ritual circumcisions. So your first priority when your therapist displays the Rabid Snarl is to satisfy yourself that he/she is not, in fact, rabid/rabid. One way to establish the absence of pathology is to kill the therapist and send selected organs to a laboratory for analysis. But since this may interfere with continuity of treatment, we recommend that you simply throw a stick out the nearest window. If your therapist responds by saying, "What motivated you to do that?" or some such thing, you can confidently rule out rabies.* If, on the other hand, your therapist bounds out of his/their chair, jumps out the window, and then brings the stick back to you, the Rabid Snarl means you should call the Humane Society without delay.

But once you rule out rabies (and lycanthropy) you will be doubly curious as to why your standard terminally neutral therapist has all of a sudden started behaving like a plaque-crazed dental hygienist. Was it something you said, or was it something he/I ate?

---

*The therapist may still turn out to be a werewolf, however, which is just one of many compelling reasons why you should carry a little henbane with you to every appointment. See my book *They Don't Call Themselves TheRapists for Nothing* (New York, The Cooperative Mutilation Press, 1982).

60

Actually it was both. The Rabid Snarl is a fluke that occurs only when you start talking about the Primal Scene (see Glossary) less than twenty-four hours after the therapist has eaten reheated meat loaf. Modern science has so far been unable to explain the dynamics of this strange cause-and-effect phenomenon, but the more prominent theorists believe that reference to the Primal Scene produces neurotransmitters, which potentiate the action of certain enzymes found only in reheated meat loaf and/or Alpo.

Whatever the explanation, the way to keep the Rabid Snarl off your therapist's face is to avoid all references to the Primal Scene until you know what she/Bernie has been eating. Of course, if you neglect this precaution and the Rabid Snarl appears, you can simply stop talking about the Primal Scene.

If the Primal Scene has never been mentioned, though, the appearance of the Rabid Snarl indicates that your therapist is a werewolf after all, and that you may be one as well.

Under such circumstances, the two of you will probably want to mate.

THE EYEGLASS REMOVAL AND BRIDGE-OF-NOSE RUB

LET'S FACE IT—your endless whining is getting on your therapist's nerves. It's reached the point where he can no longer stand the sight of you—which explains why he's taken off his glasses—and has begun to think he's developing an allergic reaction to your mere presence (if not your very existence)—which explains why he's massaging the cartilage above his sinus cavities.

As a patient, you can react to this kind of display in one of two ways. You can feel hurt and start sulking and become even whinier because your therapist doesn't like you anymore. Or you can realize, at long last, that life is no day at the beach, that Bill Buckley never promised you a rose garden, that a lot of people have much tougher lives than you do, that therapy is just one more form of self-absorption, and that real grown-ups have to shoulder their pain and take care of business without leaning on the crutch of some therapist/parent-surrogate.

If you were to realize all that, at long last, you would be well on your way to lamenting those features of life that are truly worth whining about.

And chances are very good that your formerly disenchanted therapist will join in and whine along with you.

THE JOYCE BROTHERS BLINK

THIS IS A WONDERFUL SIGN for a patient; it means your therapist is afraid of you.*

Why is that wonderful? Because you can use the therapist's fear to obtain certain therapeutic concessions. A full sixty-minute hour perhaps, or your therapist's unlisted home phone number. The Joyce Brothers Blink is your passport to wish fulfillment (see Glossary). Or maybe you'd like some extra sessions from time to time. By exploiting the Joyce Brothers Blink, you will soon be taking precedence over the therapist's other patients, all of whom are too sick to be helped anyway, really.

Be careful, however, not to confuse the Joyce Brothers Blink with a normal blink. Normal-blink therapists do not take kindly to acts of attempted coercion, and they already know all your dirty little secrets. So before you assume your therapist's blink means fear, be sure to verify that it features not only eyelash movement but a barely discernable recoil and a transient facial expression connoting panic. If *either* of these two standard concomitants is not observable, you should asssume that the blink in question is normal and that you are still the one who's frightened.

---

*But it does *not* mean that Joyce Brothers is afraid of you, or that Joyce Brothers is afraid of her own patients. In Joyce Brothers's case, the JBB means simply that Dr. Ruth Westheimer has entered the room (see The Dr. Ruth Twinkle, page 14).

THE BICEPS FLEX

LIKE IT OR NOT, there are going to be times when your therapist is in a cheerful mood. And when therapists are feeling peppy, they tend to flex their biceps.

This can be embarrassing for the patient, especially when the biceps are almost too puny to see, as in the case of many male therapists.

But why is it, you ask, that therapists should react to feelings of ebullience by flexing their biceps?

The answer lies in the deepest levels of the subconscious. After listening all day long to the endless kvetching and whining of their patients, therapists tend to experience a deep, unconscious urge to say to those patients, *"Ha!* You dorks can't get me down!"

This being so, it is but a short step to an explanation of the Biceps Flex.

Carl Jung, the great Swiss psychoanalyst, believed firmly in the crucial importance of symbols. (Of course, we now know that symbols are of absolutely no consequence whatsoever—a fact Jung might have guessed for himself had he not been Swiss.) But, secure in his misconception, he developed a symbolic language of gestures to describe the various emotional states, hoping this language might one day function as a lingua franca for therapists all over the world.

When Jung came to the feeling of defiance peculiar to therapists in a sunny state of mind, he chose what he

thought was the gesture for "up yours!" to serve as that feeling's symbolic representation.

Nutty Carl. He was wrong again. But long before he could repent of his error, his gesture-symbol language had become part of the core curriculum of every therapy school in Europe. And from Europe it crossed to the United States.

Many scholars have tried to establish the cause of Jung's confusion, apart from the fact that he was Swiss. But it wasn't until quite recently that Dr. Mendel Stench of the Hauptakademie Krankenhaus in Beutelsbach, West Germany, discovered the true story. The problem arose because Jung's primary source for the symbol-gesture vocabulary was Egyptian tomb paintings. And, of course, all the little Egyptian men in these works of art make the gesture for "up yours!" with their arms flexed out to the side.

The important point for you, the patient, to remember, however, is that whenever your therapist flexes his biceps, you should punch him right in the nose, thereby demonstrating that you're one dork who can get him down but good!

This may sound radical. But believe me, it'll make all the difference in your relationship.

"WHAT'S THE FANTASY?"

HERE YOUR THERAPIST IS encouraging you to give free rein to your filthiest thoughts and wishes, for the ostensible purpose of illuminating your unconscious mind. The true meaning of the question is, "I'm getting bored. Amuse me."

One obvious response is to go ahead and give free rein to your filthiest thoughts and wishes.

But what if it's one of those days—we all have them—when you're not constantly experiencing a need to murder, run away, violate someone, or go to the bathroom? What if, in other words, your therapist needs entertainment, and you're fresh out of material?

There's no need to panic. You can simply use the good old All-Purpose Therapeutic Fantasy, or "Apartment F," as it's known in the industry.

The All-Purpose Therapeutic Fantasy is an amalgam of certain stock elements. It should always contain sex with a member of your immediate family, a memory of bed-wetting, the fear of catastrophic humiliation, and a desire to persecute Romanians.

The most compact form of the All-Purpose Therapeutic Fantasy thus has you attempting to rape your Romanian sister and being humiliated in the process by an episode of premature ejaculation, which wets the bed to the best of your recollection. Longer versions are not only permissible but encouraged. And if you just stay with it, your own personal filthiest thoughts and wishes will soon come bubbling back into your conscious mind, where they can do the most good.

69

THE THUMB TWIDDLE

WELL, WE ALL KNOW what the thumb symbolizes. So twiddling one's thumbs is a lot like brandishing one's symbol and publicly fantasizing that one has two symbols instead of one or none. This is pretty primitive behavior, no matter what the patient may be saying. And what it means is that your therapist is temporarily out of control.

Quick action is required. First pour water on your therapist's head. Next, offer to pay in advance from now on. Last, hand your therapist a towel.

To help your therapist calm down, you may now want to intimate that it might be useful if he talked a bit about what provoked him to brandish his symbol. The therapist will probably be a little sensitive about such an horrendous loss of professional poise, so draw him out gently. Once he gets going, help him occasionally by offering interpretations of his material, and suggest a few insights as he prattles on.

Gradually you will start to feel superior to your therapist, among other people. And before long, your own thumbs will be twiddling away. This indicates that you are temporarily out of control, which will jar your therapist into once again getting a firm grip on himself.

The two of you can then resume your customary roles.

THE APPARENT YAWN

CONTRARY TO POPULAR OPINION, the Apparent Yawn is not a sign of therapist boredom or fatigue. In fact, it indicates that your therapist has unconsciously begun to identify you with his dentist.

By opening his mouth and displaying all his dental work, the therapist is saying that listening to you maunder on is roughly equivalent to having a cavity drilled.

But this is not necessarily cause for dismay, because many therapists actually enjoy having their cavities drilled. If your therapist is of that ilk, you can proceed with your therapy secure in the knowledge that the two of you have an excellent, if somewhat kinky, rapport.

If your therapist doesn't like having his cavities drilled, the Apparent Yawn means you get on his nerves. But this, too, is no problem because many patients actually enjoy getting on their therapists' nerves.

But how can you, upon observing the Apparent Yawn, determine whether your therapist likes or dislikes having his cavities drilled? Well, while the Yawn is in progress, note the dental work in the open mouth. Then swiftly stick the point of an awl into any accessible filling. If your therapist reacts with pain and indignation, you'll know you've found a secure source of sadistic satisfaction. And if the reaction is one of ecstasy,

72

you may be able to negotiate lower hourly fees.

Either way, you'll soon be a productive member of society once again.

THE LEG CROSS

WHEN A MAN CROSSES HIS LEGS, it means he feels a need to empty his bladder or protect his genitals from some symbolic threat, such as his mother. When a woman crosses her legs, it means that she is withholding the prospect of gratification and should be punished for it.

If your therapist is male, accordingly, you should respond to this action by saying very gently, "If you'd like to stop the session for a moment so you can empty your bladder, I promise I won't mutilate your genitals."

If your therapist is a woman, your response will depend on your individual sex. A female therapee, for example, can respond simply, "If you'd like to stop the session for a moment so you can empty your bladder, I'm such a worthless shit!" A male therapee, on the other hand, should react by saying, "IYLTSTSFAMSY-CEYB, you're probably frigid."

Note: I must apologize to those unfamiliar with the therapeutic focus on bodily products for including a discussion of genitals and full bladders in this volume. Perhaps, on further reflection, I may eliminate these disgusting references from the book. But I don't have time for further reflection right now. I gotta go take a dump.

THE NOSE TUG

OF COURSE, THE NOSE SYMBOLIZES exactly the same organ as the thumb, but to an even greater extent. Since most people have only one nose, however, they are unable to engage in nasal twiddling activities. Rather than twiddle, therefore, most of them tug.

You will recall that thumb twiddling is equivalent to brandishing one's real and/or fanatasized organ. Tugging on an analogous body part, accordingly, is equivalent to handling one's real and/or fantasized organ.

We're talking masturbation here.

But why should your therapist be engaging in symbolic masturbation?

Well, there's the obvious explanation: your therapist hasn't scored lately.

Then there's the almost as obvious explanation: your therapist suffers from the heartbreak of satyriasis and/or nymphomania.

Finally, there's the contrary-to-what-you-might-expect explanation: your therapist's genitals are out of order.

Whatever the real explanation, you should be careful not to become involved, unless of course you yourself haven't scored lately, in which case you should be aware that your therapist's genitals may be out of order. As long as you don't mind running that risk, go for it, by all means! Just make sure your therapist washes his hands before the two of you get started.

THE CROTCH FONDLE

THIS IS SIMPLY the Nose Tug without the symbolism.

THE WHOLE-BODY CLUTCH

AS YOU MAY RECOLLECT, the facial expression known as the Dr. Ruth Twinkle indicated that your therapist found you adorable and loved you to small pieces. The Whole-Body Clutch, on the other hand, indicates that your therapist finds himself adorable and loves himself to small pieces. This is what we call "narcissism" (see Glossary) or, in simple, everyday language, conceit.

The fact that your therapist adores himself and loves himself to small pieces shouldn't worry you unless, of course, your therapist is abnormally diminutive to begin with.

That problem aside, the feelings of self-infatuation associated with the Whole-Body Clutch are almost always transient in nature, as well they might be; and they need not frustrate your need to have your therapist concentrate all his attention on you, unless they lead him to undertake the Crotch Fondle. If you think that's where the Whole-Body Clutch is headed, a few gentle words will suffice to restore your therapist's sense of proportion. "I hear your genitals are out of order," is a surefire formula for bringing him back down to earth. And if that doesn't work, try, "Funny, you don't look Jewish!"

80

THE FINGER POINT

AS WE ALL KNOW, Pointing The Finger is the classic way of assigning blame. Thus, when your therapist Points The Finger at you, she is saying that it's all your fault she's not helping you get better.

The Finger Point tells you, in other words, that from your therapist's viewpoint, these three things are true:

1. You're not making any progress.
2. Your therapist is unequal to the task of getting you to make progress.
3. The reason your therapist is unequal to the task of getting you to make progress is that you are beyond redemption.

Now let's look at things from your side:

1. Since your therapist has already admitted she's ineffectual, it's possible she's wrong as well (i.e., about whether or not you're making any progress).
2. If she's wrong about that, it's likely she's also wrong about her inequality to the task you represent.
3. Therefore, the reason why your therapist feels unequal to the task of helping you is not that you are unsalvageable but that she is lacking in self-confidence, for reasons one can readily appreciate.

So, it follows that all you need do when your therapist Points Her Finger at you is help her get her confi-

dence back. Just say to her, "I'm OK. You're OK. *We're* OK. Indeed, the fact that we've accomplished as much as we have is amazing—especially in light of your basic incompetence."

Knowing her, she'll take this as a compliment.

"WHAT ARE YOU
FEELING RIGHT NOW?"

WHEN YOUR THERAPIST asks you this question, first check your hands. Many patients unknowingly start rubbing themselves during sessions. And many therapists want to know what's being rubbed. If you have been rubbing, answer your therapist honestly by saying, "My Cowper's glands," if that's the case, or, "My uvula," if it isn't. There's nothing shameful about touching yourself, after all. It's a lot worse than shameful.

But let's assume that you're not actually touching yourself. In this case, the therapist wants you to describe your emotional state. By doing so, the theory has it, you will make a connection between what you've been saying and the associated (masked) emotions. If, for example, you are discussing your uvula when the question is asked, and you note that what you are feeling right then is constipated, you will realize instantaneously that there is a large uncooked eggplant in your shirt pocket. This, of course, is your parents' fault, and by making the connection between your parents' crimes and the condition of your uvula, you will at long last free yourself from your ugly little eggplant fetish.

Insights like this may alter your life and may even cure you of that disgusting tendency to fondle your Cowper's glands. (If you're a woman and don't have Cowper's glands, that's your parents' fault, too.)

THE EYEBROW LIFT

WHEN HUMAN BEINGS RAISE their eyebrows, it suggests that they have their doubts about the propriety and/or credibility of a given phenomenon. Therapists are no different.

Most of the time, the Eyebrow Lift occurs in response to something you have said. But before you assume that this is the case, check the location of your hands. Is one of them fondling the therapist's crotch? If so, your words may not be all that significant.

This is simply a roundabout way of pointing out that one meaning of the Eyebrow Lift is that you are fondling your therapist's crotch.

But what if, for some reason, you aren't? What if it can only be your words that are sending his/* eyebrows, among other things, skyward? In that case, I must regretfully advise you, the news is bad.

Given all the sick filth that therapists listen to, an Eyebrow Lift reaction means that what you've just said is sicker and filthier than at least 97 percent of all patient utterances the therapist hears. In other words, you are every bit as vile and perverted as you always suspected.

Which means you've got a great future in TV evangelism.

---

*her

YOUR FINAL SESSION

THE MOMENT HAS COME. You've warded off mental health as long as possible. Your psychic energy's flowing. Self-destructive obsessions and acute regressions are things of the past. You're out there, in the world, taking care of business. And life seems richer, if a bit more bewildering.

As you and your therapist wrap things up in Your Final Session, one question will be reverberating in your skull: "Was it therapy that turned me around, or have I just matured a little over the last fourteen years?" Put another way, the question reads, "Did I really have to pay all that money?"

Although your therapist's face will be displaying only the Standard Expression of Terminal Therapeutic Neutrality, chances are the mask will conceal a good deal more emotion than usual. For even in your case, it wasn't therapy *or* maturation, but therapy *and* maturation interweaving over time that finally brought your emotional age within hailing distance of your chronological age. And if your therapist, near the end of Your Final Session, decides to have mercy on you and at long last give you a straight answer, the response you will get to, "Did I really have to pay all that money?" should not come as too much of a surprise.

"Whaddya think," your therapist will say, "I do this kind of thing for a living?!"

GLOSSARY

Countertransference The business of transporting counters. Hence, any psychic state involving a truck fetish.

Freudian slip An item of lingerie Freud wore during his drag-queen years.

Gentile Any nontherapist.

Insight That which is better than foresight.

Material Verbal information the patient offers the therapist, e.g., "I want you right now! On the floor!"

Narcissism Failure to focus exclusively on the therapist and all he or she represents.

Overcompensation Generally used to describe the salaries, bonuses, and benefits corporate executives allocate to themselves. Hence, one symptom of sociopathy.

Piss off To make someone angry or, in the case of a neurotic, petulant.

Primal scene The opening sequence of a play. Hence, the occasion on which the patient first makes payment.

Primary transference The removal of scenery from the stage after the Primal Scene. Hence, the therapist hurrying to the bank to deposit the patient's check.

Reaction formation   The pattern made by planes in an aerobatic team when their pilots notice they are all converging on a single point in space.

Regression   From the Yiddish *gres*, O.E. *grouss* + *re-* (again): A tendency to whine or complain incessantly, thereby pissing off a therapist.

Sadomasochism   Sexual intercourse among Republicans.

Secondary transference   The moment when the check clears and/or the money is credited to the therapist's account.

Simple transference   The act of paying in cash.

Sublimation   Navy jargon for antisubmarine warfare (submarine elimination). Hence, the refusal to acknowledge the existence of one's unconscious mind, thereby pissing off a therapist.

Wish fulfillment   Inner peace.